LIVING THE JESUS PRAYER

IRMA ZALESKI

NOVALIS

© 2011 Novalis Publishing Inc.

Cover design: Ingrid Paulson
Layout: Audrey Wells

Published by Novalis

Publishing Office
10 Lower Spadina Avenue, Suite 400
Toronto, Ontario, Canada
M5V 2Z2

Head Office
4475 Frontenac Street
Montréal, Québec, Canada
H2H 2S2
www.novalis.ca

Library and Archives Canada Cataloguing in Publication

Zaleski, Irma, 1931-
    Living the Jesus prayer / Irma Zaleski. -- 2nd ed.

Includes bibliographical references.
Issued also in an electronic format.

ISBN 978-2-89646-320-6

    1. Jesus prayer. 2. Spiritual life--Christianity. I. Title.

BT590.J28Z34 2011   242'.7   C2010-907962-0

Printed in Canada.

We acknowledge the financial support of the Government of Canada
through the Canada Book Fund for business development activities.

5   4   3   2   1   15   14   13   12   11

CONTENTS

PREFACE TO
THE SECOND EDITION

I was happy to learn that a second edition of *Living the Jesus Prayer* was to be published. The original version of the book was written in 1993, and the first Novalis edition appeared in 1997; it seemed reasonable to expect that, after another dozen or so years of praying the Prayer – not always very faithfully or with full attention, but never forgetting it for long – I might wish to clarify some points or make some further remarks. The editors at Novalis also suggested that I tell my readers a little more about myself and about what led me to begin the practice of the Prayer forty years ago.

I was first introduced to the Jesus Prayer in 1970 by Fr. Emile Briere of Madonna House in Combermere, Ontario. It was a difficult and challenging time for me. I had just returned to the Church after a long absence and was beginning to face the fact that I knew very little about the faith I had left behind many years before. I had no habit of prayer and belief that most people brought up in a religious family would have acquired early in life. Thus, I was an easy target for discouragement and doubt, and soon began to question the sincerity of my conversion.

I grew up in an officially Catholic but non-practising family in Poland. We hardly ever went to church and, as far as I remember, said no prayers at home. I am afraid I didn't benefit much from the religion classes I attended at school (they were obligatory in all Polish schools). I was an argumentative child and had already imbibed my father's antagonism towards the Church, along with his conviction that nothing should ever be taken on faith. I suspect the teachers enjoyed teaching me as little as I enjoyed learning from them.

My childhood ended in 1939, when the war broke out. I was only eight, but I was old enough to be aware of what was going on around me and to experience its horrors.

My father, a professional officer, escaped from Poland soon after the Germans took over; he spent the rest of the war with the Polish Army in the West. Thus my mother was left to look after my brother and me by herself in circumstances that seemed impossible to survive. The brutality – the terrible violence and cruelty that surrounded us on all sides for the next six years – made any childlike trust in the fundamental rightness of things very difficult to maintain. Life was shown to be dangerous and bleak. I became aware of the dark, at times tragic, side of human life, of the evil that so often hides in every human heart. It took me many years to face that darkness in my own being, to search for a way of coming to terms with it and, at least to some extent, to be healed. This short book reflects that search.

But that searching was a long way in the future. For the time being, we were overjoyed to be with my father and be safe. Yet we did not stay together for long. My father thought our priority must be to learn English and finish our education. As I still had two years of high school to complete, he decided to send me to a private boarding school at Dumfries, in Scotland. The school was run by Benedictine nuns.

The choice of a convent school surprised me. Indeed, it made me angry at first, given my father's hostility towards religion and especially the Church (a hostility that I had come to share). He explained that the nuns would be used to having foreign students and would know how to help me to learn the language and adjust to my new life.

He was right. The nuns were very kind and did all they could to help me learn English and make me feel at home. I was unhappy at first; I was homesick and lonely for my mother and brother, for we had never been separated for long before. Also, as I had always been an articulate child, I did not enjoy being unable to communicate easily. I was determined to learn English quickly, and soon learned enough to be able to follow my lessons, do my assignments and make friends with my fellow boarders, some of whom I still remember fondly.

Yet, it is the nuns whom I remember most. I was touched by their kindness and patience with my initial hostility and misbehaviour but, above all, by the joy and beauty of their faith – something I had never encountered before. The nuns were my first true teachers of spiritual life. They were the first to point out to me – not in words, but through their lives – the essential beauty and power of Christianity, which was so new to me. Most of all, it was there, I believe, that I had my first real glimpse of Christ. Not the sweet blue and pink Jesus I had seen in the pictures in my catechism books but of Christ truly divine, and yet also fully human and always present to us.

This religious phase of my life did not last very long, however. Once I was back living with my family and attending university, the sense of spiritual reality receded. I had returned to the world of skepticism and unbelief. I took an active part in the life of the university, argued interminably with my fellow students, and read countless books. Religion seemed like a world that belonged to the past, lost in history.

And so it was for many years. Then, in the summer of 1964, while I was staying with my two children at my father's cottage in Combermere, Ontario, I heard about Madonna House. This Catholic lay community was founded by Catherine deHueck Doherty, a Russian émigré, in 1947. I thought it might be interesting to find out more about it and so, one hot

August day, I took my children with me and walked through the Community's wide-open gates for the first time.

I was immediately drawn to the people I met that afternoon. I liked the evident simplicity of their life of hard work and poverty and their openness and kindness to all who came through their doors. They made me and my children feel very welcome; we visited them every summer we spent in Combermere. I was moved by their loving and non-judgmental religion, and by the beautiful way they prayed and sang their liturgies and celebrated their feasts. I felt deeply touched by their obvious love of God, Christ and the Church. And yet, I stubbornly refused to be drawn into their life of faith for six more years. In August of 1970, however, my resistance collapsed and I returned to the Church that I thought I had left forever. I went back to Toronto, where we lived, convinced that this time, I was back for good.

But things are never that simple. Old habits, demands of everyday living, old relationships and interests soon began to reassert themselves. Doubts began to assail me once again. It was a very painful time for me and for my family. I had to face many difficult choices, and the faith I had just embraced did not seem to make them any easier to make. I still had no habit of prayer and no clear sense of what a Christian life really was.

Above all, because I had very little understanding of the infinite, unconditional mercy of God, I had no way of accepting my own poverty and weakness without being crushed by guilt. I could not stop trying to justify myself, trying to be "good," trying to appear "blameless" before God and others, but these attempts did not help much, as they never do. They only made me feel a hypocrite and a fake. I was often tempted to become despondent and give up.

It was at this point that, on a return visit to Combermere, Fr. Briere, who knew me well by then, taught me the Jesus Prayer. This prayer was not well known or common in the Western Christian Tradition, but it was very important to the life of the Orthodox Church. Catherine Doherty (a convert to Catholicism but who was still deeply rooted in the Orthodox Tradition) introduced it to her Madonna House Community. I took up the Prayer without much enthusiasm, lacking any clear idea of what it asked of me or where it would lead me. Before too long, I began to be bored with it and perhaps resentful of the discipline it demanded, but somehow, with Fr. Briere's support and encouragement, I kept going.

And then, one day, I was surprised to discover that the Prayer seemed to be always going on within me – by itself, whether I was aware of it or not. I woke up with it in the morning and fell asleep to it at night. I realized that the presence of Christ with me and within me was becoming ever more clear to me; he was always "abiding" with me. I had begun to see that at the core of Christian teaching, and Christian life, lay the conviction, the "good news," that the Son of God, the Word made flesh – through whom and in whom the world was created – has entered our hearts, the very centre of ourselves, and abides there, whether we believe it or not, whether we are aware of it or not.

The Jesus Prayer, I discovered, was not a way of meditation *on* Christ or a path to reach some "higher" or "more spiritual" way of prayer. It was not a way of spiritual self-improvement, of acquiring merit points or becoming spiritually rich. Rather, it was the way of a beggar. To call upon the name of Jesus so often, so insistently, is to knock again and again at the door of our own hearts: "the room within." This is the deepest centre of our being, where Christ lives, an essential fact of our faith that we often forget. In praying this prayer, we remember that Christ has always been there and will never leave us, no matter what we have done, no matter how greatly we have sinned. The Jesus Prayer is, for those who embrace it, a true, healing expression of our relationship with Christ.

I know that there will always be more efforts to make, more failures to come to terms with, more doubts to endure. I shall pray the Jesus Prayer well, or not so well, many more times. And I hope and trust that, at the inevitable – and probably not very distant – moment of my death, when I see the Lord in all his power and beauty at last, I shall have the grace to remember to say it.

THE PRAYER

The *Jesus Prayer* is an ancient form of prayer, of being attentive to God who manifested himself to us in Christ. The practice of the Jesus Prayer began in the early centuries of Christianity, as a prayer of monks and nuns, the Desert Fathers and Mothers, but it was soon taught to an ever-increasing number of lay people. Also known as the Prayer of Jesus, the Prayer of the Name of Jesus, unceasing prayer, and prayer of the heart, it has been handed down to us in an unbroken tradition. Until recently, it has mainly been practised by the Eastern Orthodox Church, but is becoming known to increasing numbers of Christians in the West. It is now practised by countless men and women, lay as well as religious, all over the world.

Its form is very simple. It consists of constant repetition of just a few words: "Lord Jesus Christ, Son of God, have mercy on me, a sinner," or "Lord Jesus Christ, have mercy on me," or "Lord Jesus, have mercy," or even a single word: "Jesus." The exact wording does not matter as long as the Name of Jesus is central to it. For it is that name "that is above all names" that is our way to the centre of ourselves, the door to our "inner room" where God lives.

We practise it by sitting still, with our eyes closed, and repeating the words slowly, gently, attentively, silently, over and over again, not so much with our lips as with our minds. Some teachers of the prayer recommend that the words be synchronized with the rhythm of our breathing ("Lord Jesus Christ" as we breathe in, and "have mercy on me" as we breathe out). This helps, they say, to still the mind and allows the words of the Prayer to flow in and out in a natural way.

It is better not to worry too much about the breathing, especially at the beginning. If we practise saying the Prayer regularly, this synchronization tends to happen on its own. If we become overly concerned with the rhythm of the Prayer, this can become an obstacle to the prayer's natural flow, and may become invasive, like a fragment of a tune that goes on and on in our heads and that we are unable to stop. That is why we must not concentrate on this or any other method or technique of the Prayer, but only say the words as simply and attentively as we can. We allow ourselves to fall silent – to let the words go – whenever we need to do so. As Father Lev Gillet has suggested, we need to respect our own inner needs and find our own way of praying the Jesus Prayer.[1]

This advice applies equally to the choice of position we adopt while saying the prayer. It is best to sit up straight, for it is easier to be alert and stay awake that way. Apart from that, position does not matter. The Fathers usually stood while praying, but some sat, knelt or prostrated themselves. St. Francis of Assisi often prayed lying on his back. We should choose the position that is best for us, that makes it easiest for us to stay attentive. As we continue praying the Jesus Prayer and it begins to establish itself in us, as we begin to realize more and more to *whom* we are being attentive, we shall discover for ourselves the best position for praying it.

PRAYER OF THE HEART

The Jesus Prayer is also called *prayer of the heart*. It rises not from our physical heart, or from our ordinary mind, but from the deepest place of our being, from its very centre, from what we might call our true self. It is this inner heart that the teachers of the Prayer meant when they told their disciples that they should seek to "enter their hearts" and say the words there.

But this, I think, is not an essential part of praying the Prayer. In any case, it should not be undertaken without the advice and guidance of an experienced spiritual director. We may easily become preoccupied with the technique of the Prayer and get involved in all sorts of fantasies. We may forget that the Prayer should not be seen – for it was not intended to be seen – as a way of reaching some "higher," more exalted spirituality or knowledge. Rather, it is a way of helping us to find a real personal relationship with Christ. We are saying it *to* the Person of Jesus who is right there, with us and in us, closer than we can possibly imagine. There is no higher spirituality than that.

The presence of Jesus with us is a fact proclaimed to us by faith: Christ is with us and in us; he is above us and among us; he is in every aspect of our existence. Christ is the Word through whom we were called into being and in whom we exist. Thus we do not need to do anything to bring his presence about. All we need to do is to try and be open and attentive to it. This is true of every way of prayer, including the Jesus Prayer, if we are called to walk that way. If we keep saying the words of the prayer to Christ, to his real, full presence, we will find our true hearts without any self-conscious effort to do so. We will become aware of our hearts burning within us, just as the hearts of the disciples did on the road to Emmaus. (Luke 24:13)

Although some people may occasionally be aware of this burning as a nearly physical sensation, it is always fundamentally a spiritual experience: an inner opening of the spirit when it finds itself in the presence of God. This experience is not a sign of our advanced spiritual status, but a sign of love – our love of God, but above all God's love for us. This is the way God makes his love and presence known to us. Praying the Jesus Prayer can be for us the way of learning to be aware of God.

BEGINNING
THE JESUS PRAYER

How do we decide to begin praying the Jesus Prayer? In a way, the early teachers of the Prayer said, we do not. We are led to it by the Holy Spirit. In this sense, it can be seen as a vocation, a path of life, a response to a call that is always initiated by God. As St. Paul wrote to the Corinthians, to say "Jesus is Lord" is possible only for those who are moved to it by the Holy Spirit. (1 Corinthians 12:13) It is the result of the Spirit "groaning" in us. (Romans 8:26) So to start the practice of the Jesus Prayer – of any prayer – and above all to persevere in it, we must be drawn to it by the Holy Spirit. Each time we pronounce the Name of Jesus, we are doing so as a gift of the Holy Spirit, the fruit of our redemption. We are, in a very real sense, opening ourselves to the incarnation of Jesus in us, through the Holy Spirit. We are becoming, like the Mother of God, *God-bearers*.

How do we know that we are called to this way of prayer? In a way, we don't. If we feel drawn to try it, we should try it. It doesn't really matter what our motives are. If our motives are not pure (and whose ever are?), God will purify them. If it is not God's will for us, we shall not persevere, but if it is God's will, we shall soon know. The Jesus Prayer, like any true call, any vocation, any true love, is never imposed on us. It never does violence to our deepest spiritual desires and longings, but instead fulfills them.

Nobody else can ever tell us how we must pray. Someone may suggest a way to us. Our spiritual director, if we have one, may encourage us to try it. But, in the end, it is between us and God. There are many ways in which God may want to lead us to experience his presence in our hearts; the Jesus Prayer is one of them. If we are really drawn to it, we should embrace it gladly, but we must never say that it is the only way, or that it is a better way than others. All we need to know is that it is for us.

THE DISCIPLINE

At first, saying the prayer will cost us some effort and discipline. It is important, especially in the beginning, to set aside some time for it (perhaps just ten or fifteen minutes) every day, twice a day if at all possible. We should not be too concerned if our attention wanders, if we forget what we are saying, if we are distracted and even bored. If this happens, we just return to saying the prayer, and keep saying it through the whole period we set aside for it. We must not force ourselves beyond our limits or make an obligation of it, a burden we cannot carry. Pushing ourselves a little is all right, and at times even necessary, but we should be gentle with ourselves. To pray the Jesus Prayer is a privilege, and will soon become a joy.

We must not confuse this joy with pleasant experiences or feelings. In fact, we must not expect to experience anything, to imagine anything, to have any insights or feelings as the result of our prayer. The Prayer should not be seen as a way of reaching some higher spiritual status, but as a way of realizing that all we are and have is not of our own doing, but a gift of God's love.

> We are taught, when reciting the Jesus Prayer, to avoid so far as possible any specific image or picture .... The Jesus Prayer is not a form of imaginative meditation upon different incidents in the life of Christ. But, while turning aside from images, we are to concentrate our full attention upon, or rather within, the words. The Jesus Prayer is not just a hypnotic incantation but a meaningful phrase, an invocation addressed to another Person .... And so the Jesus Prayer should not be said mechanically, but with inward purpose; yet at the same time the words should be pronounced without tension, violence, or undue emphasis ....[2]

Also, we must not confuse the praying of the Jesus Prayer with thinking about it, forming ideas and having great thoughts. The Fathers tell us that any thoughts that come to our minds while we are praying, and there will be many – good and bad, profound and silly – are a distraction, products of our own minds. The work of the Jesus Prayer is to silence our minds and try to *just be* before the face of God. As soon as we become aware that we are thinking, however "spiritual" and "profound" our thoughts may seem to us, we should let go of them and return to saying our prayer.

This is not easy. The discipline of the Jesus Prayer, if we take it up seriously, soon loses the excitement of all new beginnings. At times, it may seem monotonous, frustrating, even boring. Our bodies do not like sitting still. Our minds do not like having to fast from thinking. Our emotions do not like being disregarded. We crave a change, some new and more exciting way of praying.

It is at such moments that we must hold on to our faith and perseverance. Perhaps we might remind ourselves that, at times, anything really worth doing seems monotonous and pointless, a grind, but only if we persevere in it can we experience the joy of its fruits. Sometimes, of course, we need a break, to take a deep breath, go for a walk, read a book, do whatever we do to relax. We shall probably find that while we are walking, reading or just breathing, the prayer still goes on in our hearts. We can't get away from it!

DISTRACTIONS

Perhaps the greatest difficulty and the greatest cause of discouragement that most of us face in our practice of the Jesus Prayer are the distractions that we seem unable to avoid. We may feel that, however hard we try, we cannot pay attention to the words of the prayer even for a minute. It is a constant temptation to conclude that we just can't do it, that this way of praying is not for us.

We may believe that a quiet setting is essential for saying the Prayer. "I think I could pray like this," we might say, "if only I had a quiet corner where I could practise it without distractions!" It is true that a peaceful setting can be very helpful to prayer. But thinking that we can pray only in a totally quiet place may be based on the illusion that all our difficulties with prayer are external. As generations of hermits have attested, most distractions do not come from outside of ourselves but from inside: from our own restless minds and souls.

It is for this reason that the teachers of the Jesus Prayer always seek to warn us of this danger and reassure us that distractions are of no importance. They are like passing waves on the surface of our minds, or clouds drifting across a clear sky – they do not ever obscure the presence of God before the eyes of our hearts. At first we must simply take this truth on faith, but eventually, God willing, we shall experience it.

Distractions, it has been said, rather than being obstacles to our practice of prayer, can become a powerful instrument of our growth in our practice. Our inattention may become the means of calling us to attention – of reminding ourselves, moment by moment, of the real meaning of the words we are trying to say, the means of our moment-by-moment conversion: of our turning away from ourselves and re-turning to God. Each time we return to the prayer, each time we become aware of how we "failed" in it, we become more aware of our weakness and of our need of God's love and mercy. We must never worry about whether we are saying the prayer well or not so well, attentively or distractedly, with energy or half-asleep. Often, after what we might consider a completely unsuccessful period of prayer, we find ourselves most at peace and closest to God. The Prayer of Jesus is always God's work in us. We just say the prayer and stay as quiet and as open as we can.

UNCEASING PRAYER

Apart from some special times we set aside for the Jesus Prayer, we may say the words of the prayer at any other moment we find ourselves remembering it. In fact, this is how many people first start on the path of the Jesus Prayer – simply saying it when they remember to say it. If we do this, we will be surprised how often these moments occur: in bed before we go to sleep, waiting for the bus, washing the dishes, having a shower, gardening, driving to work, walking. We may soon find that the words of the Prayer have penetrated our minds and hearts, and continue sounding silently within us, as if of their own volition.

Even if that never happens, if we say the Prayer only a few times a day, it will still prove to be a very great gift. The words of the Prayer will always be there for us in times of trial and distress, or when we have a difficult decision to make. They will be with us at times of great happiness and at times of great sorrow and pain. We shall be amazed to discover how very important, even indispensable – what a great source of reassurance and strength – the Prayer soon becomes for us. Eventually, we may find ourselves saying it first thing in the morning and last thing at night. We never really quite stop praying it.

This does not mean that we always shall be, or can ever be, consciously aware of the words of the Prayer, or even hear them sounding over and over in our minds. Such "constant prayer" would not be very helpful or even bearable for long. Rather, it means the words will simply be there. On some level of our minds, we will always be aware of them, of what they are telling us: Christ truly is with us and is waiting for us to turn to him.

In that the Prayer will be always with us, it will become one with the rhythm of our breathing and the beating of our hearts. It will become part of us. We shall then discover the great secret of unceasing prayer about which St. Paul spoke: "Rejoice always, pray without ceasing; in all circumstances give thanks, for this is the will of God for you." (2 Thessalonians 5:17)

THE WAY OF THE PILGRIM

The longing and search for a way of ceaseless prayer is well illustrated by a Russian story published in English as *The Way of the Pilgrim*. This story has played a key role in spreading the knowledge of the Jesus Prayer in the West. It is a tale of a simple pilgrim in nineteenth-century Russia who describes how he learned about the Jesus Prayer. He tells us that one day, when he was in church on the Feast of Pentecost, St. Paul's second Epistle to the Thessalonians was read, urging them to "pray without ceasing."

These words had a profound effect on the pilgrim. He was filled with a desire to find out how this could be done. He left his native village and travelled all over Russia. He sought out spiritual teachers and heard many sermons, but none of them could tell him how he could pray always. One day, while walking along a road, he met an old man, a monk from a nearby monastery, who invited him to come with him and rest awhile from his travels. The pilgrim thanked him, then said he did not need to rest, but to find spiritual teaching.

"What sort of spiritual teaching are you searching for?" asked the old monk. "What is puzzling you?"

"Well, it is like this, Father," said the pilgrim. "About a year ago, while I was at the Liturgy, I heard a passage from the Epistles which bade men pray without ceasing …. This surprised me very much, and I was at a loss to understand how it could be carried out, and in what way it was to be done. A burning desire and thirst for knowledge awoke in me. Day and night the matter was never out of my mind. So I began to go to churches and to listen to sermons. But, however many I heard, from not one of them did I get any teaching about how to pray without ceasing. They always talked about getting ready for prayer, or about its fruits and the like, without teaching one how to pray without ceasing, or what such prayer means. … I have not reached the understanding I longed for, and so to this hour I am still uneasy and in doubt."

Then the old man crossed himself and spoke:

"Thank God, my dear brother, for having revealed to you this unappeasable desire for unceasing interior prayer. Recognize in it the call of God and calm yourself …."[3]

The pilgrim agreed to go to the monastery with the old monk, who introduced him to the practice of the Jesus Prayer. The rest of the book tells of his experiences as the practice of the prayer took hold of him, and as he travelled across Russia on foot, visiting many holy shrines, meeting many people, and always praying the Jesus Prayer and teaching others about it.

The story of the Russian pilgrim illustrates the fact that it is very difficult to persevere on the path of prayer alone. That is why a guide, a spiritual director, or a good confessor – someone who is experienced in the difficulties and demands of the path and is willing to walk before us – can be of great help. All teachers of the prayer agree on that point. It is not easy, however, for most people in the West to find such an experienced guide. Often we must do our best on our own.

This should not discourage us or prevent us from beginning to pray the Jesus Prayer, if we are truly drawn to it. As we begin to practise the Prayer, we ask God constantly for guidance, seek others who are walking the way, and perhaps find help in reading. We remind ourselves that we can never really ever fail at prayer, for every time we try to pray, however poorly and distractedly, we make ourselves available to God.

And, above all, we trust that Christ, whose Name we constantly invoke, whose mercy we confidently expect, whose presence we long for, will guide us himself. As Mother Maria Gysi has said, "It is a journey, the soul must make it step by step and Christ leads the soul."[4]

DESIRE FOR THE PRESENCE OF GOD

The desire for ceaseless prayer is really the desire to experience the presence of God, a longing to know that, in Jesus, God truly lives in us, is always there for us. One of the great tragedies of our lives, and the lives of so many Christians, is not to experience that presence. This is why, so often, our faith does not become truly real for us. We do what is required of us, but our hearts are not touched, we do not know the joy of it.

And yet, this is why God became incarnate in Christ, why he suffered, died and rose again, why he sent us the Holy Spirit – to be always present with us. This is the meaning of the mystery of his mystical Body, the Church. This is the meaning of the sacraments, the meaning of our salvation in Jesus, of the coming of the Kingdom, of the promise of heaven. Our religion surely does not make sense unless it opens us to this immense, glorious mystery of God's presence in the world, and in our own deepest self, unless it offers us the way to enter this mystery and experience it every moment of our lives.

How can this desire for the presence of God be fulfilled? Only through prayer. This kind of prayer is usually called "contemplative" and is often considered possible only for a few chosen souls, mostly nuns and monks, and not for ordinary lay people. But this is not true. Contemplative prayer is for everyone.

I once heard a story about an old parishioner of St. Jean Vianney (the Curé of Ars) who used to spend a lot of time alone in church. St. Jean became curious about him and asked him one day, "Why do you spend so much time sitting in church? What do you think about?" The old man answered, "Oh, I just look at Him, He looks at me, and we are happy together."

This wonderful story illustrates two important points about contemplative prayer: it is not complicated, but is a simple way of being in the presence of God; and we do not have to go to the desert or enter a monastery to experience it. We can practise it anywhere, at any time. But most of us, like the Russian pilgrim, need help and encouragement to begin. We need to find a path of prayer, a simple way of experiencing the presence of God and remaining in it. The Jesus Prayer can be such a way. It can become for us a means of entering the Kingdom of Heaven, of finding heaven on earth. As Blessed Elizabeth of the Trinity has said, "Heaven is God and God is in my heart."

AWARENESS
AND ATTENTION

I t may seem that, when we talk about experiencing the presence of God, we are contradicting what has been said above: that we should not seek any special experiences in prayer, for they may prove to be not a help but a hindrance to us. They may distract us and keep us focused on ourselves, on our own thoughts and emotions, and not on God. This is true, but the experience of the presence of God in Christ of which we are speaking here is not a matter of our own thoughts, feelings or imagination. It is a matter of awareness: of becoming aware of what is real, of what is always there, but that we are usually too busy and distracted to notice and pay attention to.

The kind of awareness that the Jesus Prayer may lead us to is very simple. We do not try to imagine that Jesus is there, and even less what he looks like or what he says. We do not engage in any imaginary conversations with him. We simply try to be aware of him and attentive to him in a similar way as we are aware of the presence of someone we love in the next room, or as a mother is attentive to what her children are doing, however busy she is. We believe – we know by faith – that God in Christ is here, with us and in us. Our task is to try to remember him and be attentive to him. It is this attentiveness that is the door to our experience of the presence of God. We cannot summon this experience at will. We cannot grasp at it as if it were a possession. It is, like the Prayer itself, a gift. Ours is only a discipline of faith and perseverance. The experience, when it comes, will come of its own accord, and will be nothing like what we could ever imagine. God is immensely bigger than our imagination. Our hope is that when he comes, when he reveals himself to us in the Person of Christ, we will be able to recognize him, like the disciples recognized Christ when he visited them after the Resurrection, in ways and at times they least expected. And, then, at last, we shall know what we longed and hoped for all these years when we called on Jesus' name again and again.

REPENTANCE

When we pray the Jesus Prayer as a way of coming into the Presence of God, we should not forget that it is not always an easy or painless way. We cannot approach the infinite clarity, truth and power of God without becoming aware of the abyss that separates us. This is why, in the understanding of many of its early teachers, we cannot really undertake to practise the Jesus Prayer seriously unless we first realize our own poverty and our need of God's mercy and are willing to ask for it ceaselessly, as long as we live.

When we say the words "Have mercy on me, a sinner" – for the prayer always implies those words, even if the form we use does not include them – we must be ready to recognize that we are, in fact, sinners, in need of God's forgiveness and healing. We must also be ready to believe that God will never refuse to grant us forgiveness, that his mercy is inexhaustible. At least we must be willing to try and believe that, even if we are not yet quite able to do so. The Prayer of Jesus is a prayer of repentance. It is a prayer of sinners, not the virtuous.

At first it may be difficult to see how admitting that we are sinners could be a problem for us. Of course, we are all sinners; we have all sinned and will likely sin again. And yet, if we are honest with ourselves, we will probably find that we have all sorts of reservations. Yes, we are sinners, but surely not all the time! Haven't we been forgiven? Must we harp on our sins unceasingly? Is doing so not a sign of an exaggerated, perhaps a neurotic sense of guilt? Of doubt in God's love for us? Of a lack of humility? Or even an expression of rebellion against him who created us and who "saw that we were good"? (Genesis 1:3)

The early Christian Fathers saw this issue differently. When they talked about sin, they were thinking not so much of individual sins, of sins we have committed and may still commit. Rather, the Desert Fathers were thinking of the true source of sin: the condition of human beings who, like our First Parents, have turned away from God. They were thinking of the condition of those who are off-centre, who are not centred rightly, who are not in the right relationship with God. The root of sin – the ground from which all individual sins spring – is our alienation from God.

Repentance, then, should not be viewed, or not viewed primarily, in terms of guilt – of punishment and repayment – but in terms of *metanoia*: a Greek word meaning "conversion." We should see repentance as a way of turning away from ourselves and recentring ourselves on God. Conversion means waking up to the true reality of our condition before God and responding to this grace by returning – not just once, but again and again – to the path of holiness.

ENDLESS FORGIVENESS

When we think of forgiveness, we usually think of it as a once-and-for-all act. If we have done wrong, if we have offended or hurt another, it is right, even necessary, to ask forgiveness for it. But once we have received it, should we be expected to have to ask for it again and again? And when we are wronged by others and have forgiven them once, surely we are not expected to have to do so more than once? Yet if we reflect on this point a little more, we may understand that we cannot really forgive or accept forgiveness in any other way. We cannot forgive or be forgiven all at once.

Only God, who is infinite, who is not bound by the dimensions of time of space, can forgive sins once and for all. But we are finite. We live in time. We cannot forgive as God does. How can we forgive a terrible crime or injustice, an evil done to us or to those we love? How can we forgive childhood cruelty or abuse that may haunt us still? Could we ever forgive it at all? How can Christ ask it of us? But he has, and we must strive to understand and attempt it as well as we can.

First, we need to remind ourselves that we are not asked to condone evil committed against us or to save the evildoers of the consequences of their evil acts. We are asked only to let go of our own anger and hate. Second, we need to realize that we are not expected to forgive all at once those who have hurt us. We are not capable of such immediate and total forgiveness. Sometimes, years after we were offended or hurt, long after we thought that, at last, we had forgiven it all, we might suddenly remember it again and be overcome with fear, anger or hate. Does this mean that our forgiveness was all an illusion, that we have not forgiven at all? No. It rather means that we have not yet completed our work of forgiving. It means that forgiveness must be our constant, perhaps lifelong, task.

But we are not always merely innocent victims of someone's evil acts. We are also, and often, per-petrators ourselves. Therefore we do not only have to forgive those who have hurt us, we must also ask forgiveness from all those whom we have offended or hurt. We must accept that for them, too, it may not be possible to forgive all once. We may have to wait for their forgiveness for many years. Perhaps we will never receive it, and we must live with that for the rest of our lives. But we can never forget them. Rather, we must pray for them and ask God again and again to give them the grace to forgive us – not only for the peace of our own minds, but also for their own healing and peace.

Yet another task of forgiveness is that of forgiving ourselves. This may be the hardest task of all. To admit that we have indeed done wrong – that we have harmed another, that we are not as kind and as holy as we had thought – is very difficult for most of us, especially if we realize that we may need to do it over and over again. We need to accept and carry the burden of such endless forgiving. We need to ask Christ to teach us to forgive our pride and help us to open our hearts to forgiveness again and again. When we begin to walk the way of the Jesus Prayer, this is what we are committing ourselves to do.

WE ARE ALL SINNERS

Perhaps it will be only at the moment of death, only when we enter eternity and come face to face with the timeless, eternal love of God, that we may be able to forgive it all. This is, I think, one of the things we pray for when we pray for a "holy death." And for that, we must also wait.

We are all sinners. We are all in need of constant conversion – constant re-turning to God – because none of us can ever claim that we are truly centred, that we love God more than ourselves. None of us can say that we never think of ourselves first. To admit that we are sinners is not a question of neurotic feelings of guilt, a way of assigning blame, but a question of being real.

The reasons why we are the way we are, why we are so often imperfect, confused and unhappy, why we hurt ourselves and others, are difficult, even impossible, for us to understand. The existence of evil – in ourselves and in the world – remains an agonizing mystery, a question that often torments us. Our response can only be an act of faith, of trust in the ultimate victory of God's love in the world and in ourselves. But how hard such trust is for us when we are confronted with some great evil, some terrible act in the world, or when we are tormented by a memory of something we ourselves have done, or have failed to do!

Even more difficult to bear, for many of us, may be the constant awareness of our own ordinary lack of perfection, our failures in love, our weakness, our abysmal poverty. We often feel so shabby, so hopeless and so unlovable. Praying the Jesus Prayer, calling ceaselessly upon God's mercy, may be the only way we can face and accept the reality of who we are and learn compassion for ourselves and the world.

Forgiveness – the refusal to turn away, to hate – lies at the heart of Christian love. As Christ has told us, even "pagans" can love those who love them. (Matthew 18:21-22) The challenge of Christian love is to love those who "hate and persecute us." (Mark 11:25) It is a difficult, perhaps impossible, challenge: most often we fail. But we need not be discouraged; we never look for success. We fail, we repent, and we keep trying – always holding onto the cloak of God's infinite mercy, always calling upon the power of his Name, always remembering that our victory, when it comes, will be not ours, but his.

OVERCOMING EVIL

The Jesus Prayer may be at times a demanding way. It is very difficult to have to keep facing, again and again, our own sinfulness, the evil that is in us: our anger, our desire for revenge, our constant failure to be who Christ has asked us to be. The Prayer is a powerful weapon in our struggle with our fear of evil in our own hearts and wherever we may encounter it in the world. This struggle, as the Gospel makes absolutely clear, is the most fundamental task of every Christian.

But, as we have also learned, we must not fight against evil as the world does: by returning evil for evil, by more anger, more violence, more hate. We are called to overcome evil as Christ did, by love and forgiveness. It is not by physical suffering alone, but by forgiving his tormentors, forgiving us all, that Christ vanquished evil and destroyed the power of death, and we are to do the same.

The greatest victory of evil consists in the reaction of fear, hatred and the desire for revenge that it succeeds in arousing in those who have been wronged.

And its biggest defeat is when we refuse to react that way. The way of the Jesus Prayer is the way of overcoming this compulsion to react by surrendering all things, both good and evil, to Christ, and asking him, in his mercy, to deal with them all.

It does not matter what emotions may rage within us. Christian love is not an emotion, but a choice – an act of will. It is a way of opening ourselves to Christ's own love and mercy pouring into us and, through us, to others. When we do this, when we refuse to hate but instead surrender all evil, all wrongs, to Christ's mercy, we deprive evil of the fruits of victory. We show in our lives, in our suffering, that good is indeed stronger than evil, that love is infinitely more powerful than hate – that God can turn all evil into good.

CHRIST OUR JUDGE

Forgiving – calling on God's mercy for ourselves and for all those who have sinned against us, or against whom we have sinned – is a way of fulfilling Christ's commandment of not judging. All judgment has been given to Christ. We must not presume to claim that right for ourselves. This means above all that we must not judge ourselves. We cannot judge ourselves because we can never fully understand what goes on in our hearts. We cannot see ourselves as we truly are, as God sees us, as Christ sees us.

Does this mean that we are getting off easily? That, after all, our sins do not really matter, our wounds do not have to be lanced, our cancerous growths removed? Of course not. When we enter the path of the Jesus Prayer, we enter the path of repentance, of conversion. As we begin to walk it, with each step we become more and more aware of our own pain, our own darkness, our own sin. And that is very hard for most of us.

The way of the Jesus Prayer has been called "white martyrdom." It is the way of the Cross, because there is no greater pain than to stand in the total poverty of our human weakness, to see clearly our misery, our inability to be good. The temptation to judge ourselves, to hate ourselves, would be irresistible if we did not know and had not experienced the merciful, healing power of Jesus.

But, because we have met Christ and have experienced his compassionate, loving presence, we can surrender all judgment to him and be at peace. We can accept ourselves as we are. We can love ourselves and also love others. Because we have discovered that the judgment of Christ is not the judgment of an inquisitor or a tyrant but of a Good Physician, we are able to go to him and show him all the bleeding, cancerous places of our bodies and souls – not so he may punish us, but so he may heal us. When we stand before him and say, "Lord Jesus, have mercy on me, a sinner," we are not cringing in fear of punishment, but crying for help and healing.

The Jesus Prayer teaches us to live the great mystery of our faith, the great paradox: we are called to repent always, but never to judge; to cry for mercy but never to doubt God's forgiveness and love. The Prayer teaches us that to walk with Christ, to live in his presence, is to live in the presence of love.

ONLY GOD IS GOOD

The Jesus Prayer, because it is a path of reality, is a way of learning and accepting the tremendous truth, too often forgotten, that "only God is good." (Matthew 19:17) We cannot be good, because we do not really know what good is. We can never comprehend the nature of God's infinite goodness and infinite love. We cannot be, strictly speaking, like God. No effort of our own can ever make us so.

I think it is true to say that as we walk the way of prayer, as we become more open to God, as we grow closer to him, we become more and more aware of how great an abyss separates us from God. We begin to understand why the greatest saints seemed to mourn most deeply the fact that they were sinners. We begin, perhaps, to have a glimpse of the inexpressible longing for holiness, for wholeness, that made them so aware of their human failings – however small these may seem to us – and of their poverty before the holiness of God.

This longing, this sense of separation from God, is the heart of all true repentance. It is often a source of sadness for us, at times even of tears, that we seem to be so far away from what we have been called to be, so disappointing to ourselves and to God. But this is not a bad sadness. The Fathers often called it "bright sadness," and considered it a great gift to receive, for it brings us always before the face of God. It teaches us the meaning of mercy and fills us with joy.

Yet for us ordinary Western Christians, a full understanding of this "bright joy" may take many years to acquire, if we ever do discover it. We may have been praying the Jesus Prayer for a long time before we begin to see what we are asking for when we ask for God's mercy. We are asking for forgiveness, of course. We are asking for healing. But also – perhaps above all – we are asking for love.[5]

When we call for mercy, we are expressing the deepest longing and hope of our hearts that, however poorly we may have tried to follow the path we were called to walk, however many times we fell, eventually – perhaps only at the end – we shall really see what immense treasure was placed in our hands. We shall begin to understand that "neither death nor life, nor angels, nor principalities, nor things present, nor things to come … nor anything else in all creation, will be able to separate us from the love of God in Christ Jesus Our Lord." (Romans 8:37-39)

WORK OF LOVE

Because we cannot ever "see the heart" as God sees, we cannot really know what is good for us, and especially what is good for others. We don't know what their true needs are, what is the best solution for their problems, what would assuage their pain. But we don't need to know. The Jesus Prayer can become for us a powerful way of intercession, of praying for others. By praying the Holy Name over them, by embracing them in our thoughts and our hearts, we surrender each one of them to God's mercy and love and we trust that God will do what is best for them.

When we intercede for others in this way, when we bring them all to the mercy of Christ – the good and the bad, those whom we love and those whom we cannot love, those who love us and those who hate us – we do what the Lord has told us to do and what he himself did on the cross. This is the great way of love to which he has called us, and also is our work, the only work that truly matters, the work of love.

We sometimes worry that we are not doing enough, not sharing enough, not serving the poor, visiting the sick, or performing other works of mercy. And, of course, it may very well be true. In order to be faithful to the Gospel, to fulfill the commandment of love, we must do what we can for each other. Without doing that, we cannot call ourselves Christ's disciples.

On the other hand, we often forget that our good acts will not bear much fruit, will not give life, if they are not performed out of love. And we cannot make ourselves love. Loving is a gift, the fruit of prayer, of opening our hearts to God. When we pray for others, we begin to love them as Christ loved them, and we do the work he commanded us to do. If there is more we need to do, he will show us in his own good time.

By praying the Jesus Prayer over each human being we meet, by pronouncing the Holy Name over everything we do, over the whole natural world, over the whole creation, we become instruments of their sanctification, channels of the Holy Spirit, bearers of the fire of Divine Love.

PERFECT ACT OF LOVE

The Jesus Prayer has also been compared to Holy Communion. The Prayer is a way of spiritual communion with Christ, of participation in his perfect act of love. By repeating the Name of Jesus, the Divine Word, we surrender ourselves totally to him; we throw ourselves completely on his mercy; we unite ourselves with him. We become aware that in a deep, true sense, we, like St. Paul, can also say, "I live, but no longer I, but Christ lives in me." (Galatians 2:20)

The implications of this truth are greater than what our minds can ever grasp or imagine. It means that all our lives, everything we do, say, think – everything we are, if surrendered to Christ – becomes united to him and is, in a profound sense, a sign of his action and his Spirit. It means that all reality is sacramental, a sign of God's presence in the world, and that every moment of our lives, all our tasks – "our duties of the moment," as Catherine Doherty used to say – are a prayer and therefore sacred.

When we pray the Jesus Prayer, we become like the disciples. We are the disciples who, at the Last Supper, heard the priestly prayer of Jesus for the first time. We realize that it is for us he prays that we may be "established in his Name," and glorified with him. (John 17) The priestly prayer of Jesus belongs, of course, to the whole Church, but perhaps, in a very special way, it belongs to those who are trying to surrender their whole lives, their whole being, to the power of the Name that the Father gave to his Son, and that lives in them.

When we are established in Christ's Name, we are being glorified with him, we are becoming like him, we are becoming him – another Christ. In the language of the Eastern Christian Tradition, we are being "divinized." As we continue to pray the Jesus Prayer, day after day, year after year, this tremendous truth penetrates our whole being, and our lives become more and more centred on it.

THE OFFERING

When we pray the Jesus Prayer, we stand empty-handed, having nothing of ourselves to offer, and expecting everything from God. That is why this Prayer has been compared to the Eucharist. This does not, of course, mean that it is of the same nature as the Eucharist, or that it could ever be viewed as a substitute for the Eucharist, but only that it resembles it in one respect. The Eucharist is the great, incomparable sign of the mystery of salvation and it is always the work of God.

At the Eucharist everything is done *for* us, everything is offered *to* us, we cannot lay claim to having any part in it, except the offering of ourselves. We often find it difficult to accept this truth, because it seems to imply that nothing we do is of any value, and that we must remain totally passive in the work of our redemption. Everything we have to offer, everything we call "I" is so poor, so infinitesimally small in comparison to what we are receiving, that we hardly dare to offer it at all.

And yet, this offering of ourselves, however small and worthless it may seem, is of infinite value because it constitutes our part in the work of salvation. It is our work: our part is not passive, but a vigorous taking up of our poor selves and offering them up to the mercy of God. It is an act of faith and therefore an act of thanksgiving, a "Eucharist," a hymn of praise and thanksgiving for the mystery of salvation in Christ. Even a glimpse of that mystery makes our hearts overflow with gratitude and awe.

When we pray the Jesus Prayer, we ceaselessly proclaim the same mystery, and offer the same worship of gratitude and awe. As the Letter to the Hebrews expresses it, offer to God, through Jesus, " a continual sacrifice of praise, that is, the fruit of lips that confess his Name." (Hebrews 13:15)

WE MEET GOD ALONE

There is still another dimension of the Jesus Prayer. Why, when we say the Jesus Prayer, do we say "have mercy on *me*, a sinner"? Why "me" and not "us"? Should we not pray for mercy for everybody? Should we not pray for the whole Church? Of course we should. In a very real sense, we can only pray within the Church. When we say "Jesus," and ask for his mercy, we ask on behalf of his whole body, the Church, and by implication, on every human being who has ever lived. (See also Romans 8:12.)

On the other hand, because the Jesus Prayer is a prayer of repentance, a prayer of a sinner, it must also be a prayer of each one alone. We still need to say, "Lord Jesus Christ, have mercy on *me*, for *I* am a sinner!" In the final analysis, we must make our own individual peace with God, find our own relationship with Christ, meet him face to face. Nobody can do it for us. Somebody can bring us to Jesus, but we must meet him ourselves. And nobody can ask forgiveness for our sins and be forgiven, but ourselves.

In this respect, too, the Jesus Prayer resembles the sacraments. We cannot be baptized by proxy, or go to confession for anybody else; neither can we receive communion or any other sacrament for anyone but ourselves. We say, "Jesus, have mercy on me," just as we say before communion, "Lord, I am not worthy to receive you, but only say the word and I shall be healed." We receive communion within the Church, but we must open our hearts to its presence alone.

DOOR TO COMMUNION

This fundamental aloneness of the human being before the face of God is very difficult for many of us to accept. We often associate it with loneliness, with lack of love and rejection, even with death. We are disappointed and filled with anxiety when we discover that even in our closest human relationships, in our moments of deepest love, we can never really dissolve the boundaries that separate us from others. For most of us, this is a frightening realization. We probably try to escape our aloneness in every way we can. We fill each moment of our lives with every possible distraction, every image, every noise we can think of. We hardly ever feel comfortable with silence.

We often carry over this fear into our relationship with God and our prayer life. And so, we run from one devotion to another, from one spiritual book to another, from one prayer group to another. We scatter ourselves all over the spiritual map. We are never still. We forget, or perhaps we have never learned, that although we can never break down the walls of our aloneness ourselves, God certainly can. Our aloneness – our separateness – is not a prison in which we must remain forever, but a door to communion: with God, but also with the whole universe. For God brings with him every human being who has ever lived.

Praying the Jesus Prayer can become such a door for us. By praying it simply, standing alone and totally open and real before the face of Christ, we become aware of the great silence – the holy silence – at the heart of our being, the silence behind the distractions, the noise, the emotions that assail us from all sides. By repeating the Name of Jesus over and over again, by patiently putting away from us all distractions, all our own thoughts and feelings, our minds become emptied, purified, ready to receive the gift of silence, the gift of being still.

HOLY SILENCE

True silence is a great gift of God, and we should pray for it every day. It allows us to experience and hear the voice of God, who lives in our hearts and is speaking to us. He is always there, and he is always speaking to us, but the outer and inner noise that usually fills our lives prevents us from hearing him.

But true silence is not merely an absence of noise, an external, physical silence, although of course that lack of noise is also very important and at times necessary. True silence, the silence that the Jesus Prayer seeks to establish in us, is, above all, an inner silence, a silence of the heart.

True silence is the search of man for God. True silence is a suspension bridge that a soul in love with God builds to cross the dark, frightening gullies of its own mind, the strange chasms of temptation, the depthless precipices of its own fears that impede its way to God. Such silence is holy, a prayer beyond all prayers, leading to the final prayer of constant presence of God, to the heights of contemplation, when the soul, finally at peace, lives by the will of him whom she loves totally, utterly, and completely.[6]

To become still in order to hear God, to experience his presence, to be established in his silence, is the true aim of all Christian prayer. Christian prayer is never a program of self-improvement, raising one's consciousness or becoming enlightened. Neither is it – at least not primarily – a list of petitions and requests for ourselves or others. Christian prayer is always and above all a *relationship*. It is turning away from ourselves and embracing God in Christ.

Prayer is a path of self-denial, of *kenosis*, a Greek word that means "emptying." St. Paul used this word about Christ in his letter to the Philippians (2:6-11). Prayer is a path of stripping ourselves of all that is not God, of becoming poor in heart so God can fill us with himself; then we can experience his presence and be one with him. This is also the aim of the Jesus Prayer. Every time we call upon the Name of Christ, we turn away from ourselves and re-turn towards him, the source and Lord of our being. While we are still on earth, we are already beginning our life in heaven.[7]

PRACTICE FOR DEATH

The Jesus Prayer puts us in the spiritual space in which we shall find ourselves at the moment of death. We die alone. The only other person there who will really matter at that moment will be Jesus: our Lord, our God and our judge. We shall have left everyone and everything else behind. We shall have crossed the boundary that separates life from death. We shall be judged according to heavenly measures, which, in this world, we cannot even begin to comprehend – by Perfect Love, in the face of which we shall have nothing to offer but our weakness, our failure to love, and our repentance.

We shall then, perhaps for the first time, truly understand the glory and the joy of repentance. We shall fully understand that in the presence of the perfect, inexhaustible love of God, we can never do anything but pray for mercy, and we never need to do anything but pray for mercy. At the end, all of us, saints or sinners, are like the repentant thief: we enter Paradise only through the mercy of Christ. When we realize this, we can truly rest; we will finally find peace.

The coming of that day, of our meeting with Christ face to face, is the only absolute certainty we have about the course of our lives. That day is already present in the mind of God. For God, all events of human life, every moment of time, is also an event in eternity, part of the eternal now. Thus, for God, our end is already known. His judgment has already been pronounced, and our cry for mercy has already been heard. God's mercy has already flowed down on us and covered our wounds and misery. We have already been forgiven. We have already been raised from the dead. The Jesus Prayer places us in the reality of that moment, in the place of that meeting. When we say the Jesus Prayer, we are saying it for our end. In a very real sense, we are practising for death.

This does not refer only to actual, physical death. Every Christian's life must also be a way of self-denial, of the daily death of self, because we must die to self in order to rise with Christ to new life. The Jesus Prayer, because it is a way of *kenosis* – of emptying ourselves of self – is also the way of the death of self. Each time we call on Jesus to have mercy, we surrender ourselves to him. We accept his judgment and meet him in the "peace of the end." By praying the Jesus Prayer, we are facing the fear of the end, but also beginning to experience the "indescribable and glorious joy" of our resurrection. (1 Peter 1:3-9)

HYMN OF JOY

In the language of faith, joy is not a merely human emotion but the fruit of the Holy Spirit, a grace. Joy is a spontaneous response of the human soul when, stripped of all its illusions and all its conceits, the soul is able to step out of the prison of its own ego and finds itself in the presence of God. This is why, I think, those who have learned the secret of ceaseless prayer and ceaseless conversion – the saints – are so often icons of joy. For, as Catherine Doherty liked to say, a sad saint is a contradiction in terms.

The Jesus Prayer, we are taught, is a great hymn of joy, because it is a way of coming into Christ's presence – the source of all our joy – and experiencing his love and mercy every moment of our lives.

Often we come to Christ sad, bowed down by our own sin, our loneliness, our self-doubt or even self-hate. But we also come – surely not often enough – in moments of joy and delight, in the everyday, simple events of our lives. We share all we have with him. We call upon his Name, we look up at his face and see that we have nothing to fear. We know that Christ will always be there for us, that he will rejoice in our joys and support us in our sorrows. We know that he will never reject or condemn us, that he will never get tired of forgiving and loving us. We are filled with hope that he *will* save us, *will* draw us away from the unreality of sin into his own glorious reality.

Our cry for mercy is a cry for healing and an expression of our faith and joy in the knowledge that although we are helpless to save ourselves from our preoccupation with self, from our fears, from our sin, God will do it for us. He himself will bridge the abyss that separates us from him – indeed, he has already bridged it in Christ. The Jesus Prayer is our hymn of gratitude for the gift of salvation in Jesus. The Fathers and Mothers who first taught the Prayer called it a summary of the whole Gospel. The words "Lord, Jesus Christ, Son of God, have mercy on me, a sinner" are our joyful confession of faith in the truth of our salvation.

LIVING THE JESUS PRAYER

All that we have been taught about the Jesus Prayer, all that we have learned and experienced through it, will make us realize that it is much more than a practice, a form of prayer and discipline. The Jesus Prayer is a way of life.

Of course, it is a practice, too. We need to make the effort, to acquire the discipline, the habit of it. We struggle with its monotony, its demands to put away our own thoughts and feelings. We deny ourselves. We carry our daily cross of trying to do God's will and seeing more and more clearly how often we fail. We resist the temptation to judge ourselves, to judge anybody, to fight evil with its own weapons. But, in the end, we make the effort, accept the discipline and take up our cross because we realize that it brings us life, that it is our life, the life we have been called to. We *live* the Jesus Prayer.

Praying the Jesus Prayer, we strive to enter a new world, a world of the real, constant presence of the risen and glorified Christ. We strive to live our lives, moment by moment, in a relationship with him. If we persevere, then one day we shall perhaps open our eyes and see that, indeed, we have found the hidden treasure, the pearl of great price – that we have already entered the Kingdom.

As has been said again and again, this life of intimate, constant, unceasing relationship with Jesus is not a question of thoughts or feelings but of faith, and therefore it is always a gift of God. There may be moments when we actually experience the reality of our life with Christ. These moments are a great joy, a special grace, a glimpse of heaven. But the essential thing is to keep that deep, central space of our being that we call the heart wide open and turned towards him. The Jesus Prayer leads us into that space, and allows us to live there with him unceasingly.

The great teachers of the Eastern Christian Tradition spoke, with the boldness of their great faith and love, of the *divinization* of each human person, of being transfigured into that divine image we were created to be. For those who are led to it and have the grace to persevere, the Jesus Prayer, the Eastern teachers assure us, can be a path up the mountain of Transfiguration. With God leading us, we, too, may one day be able to reach the top of the mountain, the goal of our journey, the place of our end, where we shall see him as he truly is, and become like him for all eternity.

NOTES

1 A Monk of the Eastern Church (Lev Gillet), *The Jesus Prayer* (Crestwood, NY: St Vladimir's Seminary Press, 1987).

2 Bishop Kallistos Ware, *The Orthodox Way* (Crestwood, NY: St Vladimir's Seminary Press, 1986), 164.

3 *The Way of the Pilgrim*, translated by R.M. French (New York: Seabury Press, 1968), 5–7. A new translation of the book by Olga Savin (with an introduction by Fr. Thomas Hopko) was published by Shambala in 2001.

4 *Mother Maria, Her Life in Letters*, edited by Sister Thekla (London: Darton, Longman & Todd, 1979), 49. Mother Maria (Lydia Gysi), a spiritual teacher and writer, was the foundress of the Orthodox Monastery of the Assumption at Normanby, North Yorkshire, England. She died in 1977.

5 As Archbishop Anthony Bloom used to point out, the word "mercy" – *eleison* in Greek – could be seen as related to the word for "anointing" with oil (a common Greek way of healing). It is also interesting that in Slavic languages, the root of the word "mercy" is also "love."

6 Catherine Doherty, *Poustinia: Christian Spirituality for Western Man* (Notre Dame, IN: Ave Maria Press, 1974). In this, her best-known work, the foundress of Madonna House Apostolate explains Eastern Christian spiritual tradition to Western Christians. (*Poustinia* is a Russian word meaning "the desert.") Although her subject is not the practice of the Jesus Prayer as such, she refers to it repeatedly and puts it in the context of living the life of love, of total surrender to God.

7 This "life in heaven" should not be confused with any emotion, however good and even holy it may appear to us. We should never forget how easy it is to fall into all kinds of spiritual illusions or "highs" at the beginning of any spiritual path. Every experienced spiritual teacher would warn us of that danger. It is better to be wary of these moments and not to rely on them. They will quickly pass.